OPEN QUESTIONS IN WORSHIP
Gordon Lathrop, General Editor

How does worship evangelize?

Mark Olson
Frank Senn
Jann Fullenwieder

Augsburg Fortress
Minneapolis

OPEN QUESTIONS IN WORSHIP
How does worship evangelize?

ISBN 0-8066-2800-6
ISSN 1080-0565

Copyright © 1995 Augsburg Fortress. All rights reserved. Except for brief quotations in critical articles or reviews, no part of this book may be reproduced in any manner without prior written permission from the publisher. Write to: Permissions, Augsburg Fortress, 426 S. Fifth St., Box 1209, Minneapolis, MN 55440-1209.

Scripture quotations, unless otherwise noted, are from the New Revised Standard Version Bible © 1989 Division of Christian Education of the National Council of the Churches of Christ in the United States of America. Used by permission.

Cover and interior design: Ann Elliot Artz
Cover photo: Ann Elliot Artz, a private garden, Island of Torcello, Italy

Manufactured in the U.S.A.   10-28006

99   98   97   96   95   1   2   3   4   5

CONTENTS

Foreword	4
What is evangelism? *Mark Olson*	6
What is leadership in worship and evangelism? *Frank Senn*	14
How does the liturgy inclusively share the Christian faith? *Jann Fullenwieder*	22
Afterword	30
For further reading	32

FOREWORD

Here is a question of current urgency and widespread discussion in the churches of North America and the world. Here, within these covers, are several clear voices to join that discussion.

Remember, this series of books is addressing *open questions*. That is, given an assembly centered in and living from word and sacraments, how may we freely discuss the things which are *not* given, about which we may have different answers? For example, *how do we welcome people* to such a community that, every Sunday, reads and preaches *scriptures* as an encounter with the risen Christ, remembers or holds that *holy bath* in the grace of the triune God, and celebrates the *meal* that proclaims the Lord's death until he comes? Are these things only for believers? Or do they speak the gospel of Christ, the "evangel," to strangers and "outsiders" too? How does a congregation that finds these central things to be its very life do evangelism? And, *do these central things themselves evangelize*, do they bring the newcomer to faith? Is there a liturgical or sacramental evangelism?

Such questions are partly practical and strategic (what shall we do?) and partly theoretical (what do we mean?). The responses of the authors here are both. Mark Olson helps us think before we begin too quickly to plan. "What is evangelism?" he asks. His answer is situated, with clear intention and some passion on his part, within a current debate on "needs-based" evangelism and, therefore, on "seeker-centered" worship. He wants us to ask whether it is right to "market" the gospel of Christ—or the program of the church—to a current perception of the needs of a "target population." What else might be the starting place for evangelization? Who else might it be for? And how does the answer to these questions affect the nature of the worship of the community?

Frank Senn offers quite concrete help to congregational planning and to the various persons who actually serve in worship. Starting with the given worship of the assembly in word and sacrament, he suggests ways in which the leadership of the congregation will continually make this center evangelically available. In the process, his strong, constant theme is this: the worshiping congregation itself is a primary witness to God in our world.

Evangelization, when it is about welcoming people to the community of faith, is always about inclusivity. The danger is that many so-called evangelism efforts are, instead, about welcoming people just like us to our club. How is that to be avoided? Jann Fullenwieder proposes an answer to that question by taking us to the most central matters of Christianity—to the Bible, to the doctrine of the Trinity, and to the "first things" of worship. In the process, she invites us into the "inclusivity of God," into the "catholicity of Jesus."

Welcome to this collection of essays that propose that the *word and sacrament* at the heart of the life of the church *are evangelical* and are the source of all true evangelism. And, in this company, welcome to your own ongoing thought about how that is so and what your own parish might do about it.

Gordon Lathrop
General Editor

What is evangelism?

Mark Olson

Evangelists invite people, both congregational members and those yet to be members, more deeply into Jesus Christ and the community that bears his name.

Is that right? Is "inviting people into Jesus Christ" going to work in our modern consumer world? Isn't a definition like that old-fashioned? Don't we have to adapt that almost embarrassingly simple message into words and ways that meet people today? Is it not true that the first step in "effective" evangelism is "knowing the people we are seeking to evangelize?"

Of course, today's effective evangelists work very hard to shape their invitation to meets the needs of the people to whom it is addressed. Similarly, it seems, effective evangelizing congregations shape their program so that it meets the perceived wants of those who are invited. That is simply the way it is done. We uncritically believe effective evangelism focuses on knowing people and their context.

As a result, we become congregations that seek to be "relevant" to the seeker. "Come here," we often say. "Here you will get your wants met. Here we will give you just what you think you need—whatever that is: entertainment, classes, kindness, child care, anything. Just come."

And they do come. For a time they come shopping at the spiritual mall. As these modern shoppers seek out what they think they need, they find acceptance and belonging. For a time it works until the aerobics classes and the "mothers' day out" lose meaning. They come for a time until they are again forced to face the spiritual vacuum that lies just beneath the surface of their lives. Then they are lost again.

What's wrong? Has the church focused on the wrong things? Do we need to re-imagine what it means to be evangelists?

Our context—our mirror

Evangelism would be simple if, in truth, we were dealing with a world of relatively well-adjusted people who simply need to find spiritual filler for the small cracks in their lives, their relationships, and their future. But we are dealing with a broken, frightened, lonely, desperately disappointed people. Most terrible of all, the face on "them" is our own face.

We may ignore this truth, but it will not go away: In our world fear holds us captive. Violence, expressed in more ways than just physical lashing out, forces us to build secure walls around ourselves and those we love. In our fear, we close ourselves off from anything different, strange, or troublesome. Only those things we know and understand can be trusted. Keeping things the way they have been becomes our highest value. We lock the doors and windows tight and carefully manage life to provide the illusion that we are safe.

Shame marks our lives. Shame differs from guilt. Guilt arises from what we do; shame arises from who we are. As individuals and as a society we are ashamed of what we have been (e.g., U.S. involvement in Vietnam), who we are (e.g., escalating violence), and where we are going (e.g., environmental and nuclear despair). We act out, individually and collectively, our shame in anger, depression (anger turned inward), and violence. Remedies like increased legal demands and higher expectations only increase the shame. We know it should be different, but we are powerless to break the cycle of shame that continues and intensifies.

Disappointment prevails more than we care to admit. The promises of the modern age have failed us in many ways. Modernity asserted that if we could just learn everything we needed, we could fix all that was broken. Human potential set the agenda. Yet, the great paradox remains that as our knowledge and ability have increased, the quality of our life has not improved. For example: In an age of tremendous medical breakthroughs, AIDS now touches, directly or indirectly, almost everyone's life. The great promises of technology have not only resulted in much good but have also produced a monstrous nuclear threat and ever more resourceful and dangerous terrorists. Our disappointment expresses itself in the unwillingness to believe or trust any promise made. Many people are cynical about almost any hope. We are wary of institutions, relationships, and even long-held religious convictions. Most painfully, we experience disappointment with ourselves. We are a people plagued by unfulfilled promises, and we are unable and unwilling to trust little beyond our own limited manageable sphere.

Loneliness keeps us empty. Ashamed, we are too humiliated and angry to reveal ourselves to others. Let down, we will not trust again. We don't like being alone, so those of us who have the money create safe technological relationships that give the illusion of being connected with others (TV, E-mail, shopping malls, and so forth). Yet, we long for more. We want and need community but no longer know how to make it happen. We have a deep desire to be in relationship with others but do not have the internal resources to fulfill the desire.

Let there be no doubt about it, the people described above are not just those who are outside the community of faith. This depiction applies both to congregational members and to those who are not members. We cannot escape our context. Consequently, evangelical activity, if it is to have credibility, must be addressed to all. *When evangelism applies only to those outside the community of faith, the gracious gift of transformation in Christ becomes trivialized into a campaign for new member recruitment and institutional growth.* Even more, when the Christian community and its leaders refuse to hear their own invitation, they become preoccupied with themselves and cut off from the source of life. We all need to be evangelized again and again. We need to hear the message because we too are afraid, ashamed, disappointed, lonely.

The evangelical dilemma

Evangelists offer an invitation leading to change, transformation, and adventure. The very essence of the invitation of the gospel conflicts with the deepest hurts of those for whom the invitation is extended. Evangelists face the dilemma of offering an invitation that no one seems ready or able to embrace. Again, this predicament applies not just to those outside the community, but to all.

Of course, the first reaction has been to adapt the invitation and make it "relevant." The mandate "to bring the gospel to the world" has been taken as a challenge for the church to know the culture, understand its hurts and hopes, listen carefully and empathetically, and then find ways to meet the needs that surface. Both congregations and evangelism leaders have followed this course of action. As a result the church's agenda—its pastoral mission—has been formed by the culture. In fact, many in the churches have come to believe that the culture (both inside and outside the community of faith) must bless the message and its presentation with a positive response or the message itself is not faithful. Quantitative measuring devices (membership, worship attendance, financial support, the number of people served) are taken to determine the effectiveness of the message. The validity and authenticity of the invitation now depends on the response of the hearer.

Thus, churches commonly seek to attract people by meeting needs and by providing the "commodity" most sought after (and revenue producing!). Sociological tools like market research, needs analysis, and program development become the primary evangelism resources. Creating a "user friendly" environment by focusing exclusively on the "client" or "consumer" (potential members) becomes a first step for the evangelist. Congregations lure people with promises, both implicit and explicit, of a better life, more happiness, affirmation, new friends (who are just like you), and all the "how to" courses you can imagine. Evangelists promote a place where people are coddled, cared for, and affirmed. "Come to church," we say, "and find a place where all that is broken can be fixed. In the midst of a hostile world, come to place where you are what is most important and everyone is nice."

People do respond to the message. In a culture full of fear, shame, disappointment, and loneliness, a "marketing" approach initially works. Soon, however, the initial rush to accept the invitation leads to more fear, shame, disappointment, and loneliness. It cannot be otherwise, for the implied promise of "fulfillment" relies on human efforts. The invitation calls for involvement in yet another human institution marked by its own failures and brokenness.

Soon, the church confirms the fear fostered by a violent world. People mistreat one another. Broken trust and misconduct abound. Lack of attention or an unintentional misdirected word or action triggers anger, depression, or violence. Unfulfilled promises lead to more disappointment, cynicism, and lack of trust. Finally, because people have accepted the invitation to come and have their needs met, loneliness increases. People come expecting to be the focus of attention. Each of them has the most important need that must be filled. *Authentic relationships, which demand attention to others, are impossible when people perceive themselves as consumers and others as vendors.* The invitation, adapted to meet the needs of the world, which at first seemed so right and worked so well, now accomplishes the opposite of what it intends.

Evangelism that seeks to bring the gospel to the world by acquiescing to the world in a quest for relevance results in driving the world away and offering nothing new. In fact, those who promote such a view of evangelism simply reproduce thinly veiled models of evangelism from another cultural period (e.g., nineteenth-century American frontier revivalism). This invitation offers us more of what already draws us to despair.

At the most profound level, this approach fails. For all people long to escape the ultimate source of fear, shame, disappointment, and loneliness: death. No matter the number of "how to" classes offered, "Christian" aerobics sessions held, or entertaining rallies planned, 100 percent of all people die. Even Jesus died, a truth often not mentioned in churches seeking to meet people's needs. In the face of death, belief that life is fixable shatters. From death there is no escape.

The evangelical dilemma of witnessing to the gospel contrary to the perceived needs of people must not be resolved through accommodation to the people. The present challenge involves sending evangelists with the true "evangel."

The evangel

There is but one place to begin to address both the brokenness of the world and the misdirection of the church. There is one "evangel": God, revealed in Jesus Christ. Evangelism originates in Jesus' action in and for the world. All invitations to enter more deeply into Jesus and the community that bears his name mirror the invitation offered in Jesus' death on the cross.

To begin at any other place will inevitably lead in confusing directions. All offers of welcome to the church and its ministry must clearly connect with the gracious welcome of God through Jesus. When the connection to Jesus is absent, the invitation becomes nothing more than yet another request to consume another product among the many that plague our lives with unfulfilled promises.

Yes, Jesus merits the title of evangel. Yes, the subject of evangelism must be Jesus, the crucified one. But, who speaks for Jesus? Who proclaims his name? How is Jesus Christ made known?

The witness to Jesus happens through the community of faith. In word and sacrament, the truth of Jesus Christ is set forth and the community is continually reformed around that truth. People enter discipleship by entering a community of people who are baptized into Christ and live out their lives— with each other and in service to God and stranger—in a particular way. The church has been named the body of Christ. It is what it eats in the holy supper. The gathering of people who claim Jesus as Lord are the most visible—not the only, but the most visible—expression of God's activity in the world. Called, gathered, enlightened, and sanctified by the Holy Spirit, the congregation shows to the world a vision of the reign of God. The language of the congregation, both verbal and non-verbal, invites (or fails to invite) others into a relationship with this vision and this reign.

More specifically, there are those the congregation has set apart to be explicit in their proclamation. For some Christians, evangelical witness may be implicit in gracious actions for others, actions rooted in the community's vision of the reign of God. These actions may still remain vague to the recipient. But others cannot be ambiguous in their witness. In the name of the evangel and the community shaped by Christ's sacramental presence, these people cannot be silent. They boldly speak the name of Jesus. Pastors and others set apart by the community must make the implicit action or word explicit. There can be no doubt who is the subject of the "good news." The name of Jesus must be named.

Invitation to covenant

Evangelists *invite*. That word connotes the graciousness and hospitality that mark the activity of evangelism. Yet, the word can distort an essential quality of evangelical activity. The image of "invitation" does not always convey the urgency and compelling depth of the offer made by the evangelist.

Evangelists *offer a covenant*. The covenant originates in God's passionate desire to be in relationship with all that has been created. In a covenant both parties become vulnerable and willingly enter a relationship full of risk. God has been offering this covenant since the beginning of creation. The relationship, though often strained and broken by humankind, has not been severed. The biblical story tells of God's continual commitment to be in covenant with the beloved creation. The full expression of God's turning to the world, summing up all covenants, is the sending of Jesus. In this evangelical act, God invited—made a new covenant—with the world. The passion and death of Jesus reveal the depth of God's desire to be in relationship with all creation.

To be in a relationship means to be on a dynamic adventure. Entrance into a covenant means change for all parties involved. The one who offers the covenant and the one who receives the gift both change. The adventure of covenant means risk and transformation. A static, unchanging relationship is an oxymoron.

Thus, the invitation offered by the evangelist (Jesus, the congregation, the pastor, and others) summons people to vulnerability and change. As the new relationship is forged, evangelists will not be surprised by the changes that enter their lives. *Covenant-making involves transformation. Those who are invited must be warned.* The covenant being offered them calls them to death and resurrection. The offer to join a particular community must not be reduced to a meeting of perceived needs. Joining in a covenant moves people from being mere consumers into a dynamic relationship of discipleship. The community of faith is a not a vendor of divine truths, dispenser of programs, or outlet for inspirational entertainment.

Evangelists offer the invitation to be in relationship. The offer must have integrity. Those being invited to covenant must know, from the very beginning, they will be changed and made new in the course of time. Those offering the invitation must also be open to the gift of transformation given in and through the stranger.

The evangelical possibility

Evangelists today must set aside the modern call to bring the gospel to the world and instead invite the world into the gospel. This change of focus means the evangelist—clearly defined by the message—takes a stand and boldly trusts the invitation itself. The evangelists must trust that people's *deepest* needs, including their own, will be met only through entering into a covenantal relationship with God as God is known in Jesus Christ.

Evangelism understood in this way demands that all ministry will be *a mediated ministry*. Direct, intimate, and immediate affinity between people—though it appears appealing—will always disappoint us. Only relationships received as gifts of the crucified and risen Christ can withstand the brokenness inherent in our lives. Only a promise not silenced by death can provide courage to trust again.

Because the new relationship invites people on a path that will lead to transformation, the path itself will hold risk, danger, and trial. Doubt, fear, and reluctance will often attend this pilgrimage. The doubts and fears, however, are not the focus of the journey. Invited to relinquish ourselves to the vision of the gospel, we discover hope and courage. When no longer a customer or client, people are liberated as they give themselves away. When removed from the center of attention, people have room to explore, imagine, and experience hope coming from beyond them.

The contemporary compulsion to focus on meeting needs and developing unmediated relationships has become an unbearable burden. All the weight of the world and its problems now are focused on each person. No wonder we often feel "victimized" and "abused"—in the most profound way, we are.

Evangelism today demands the courageous conviction to announce a vision of hope beyond the perceived needs of people. Evangelists must trust the vision of the gospel as set forth in the tangible, graceful means of word and sacrament and boldly offer it as hope for the world. Evangelism in our culture will be truly good news when we invite people into the gospel of the crucified and risen Jesus.

Worship and evangelism: implications

1. Worship, which most clearly defines a faith community, must announce what is central to the community. Even, or maybe especially, what is most challenging and offensive to the dominant culture must be made visible. For Christian worship this means Jesus, the crucified Savior, must stand at the center of what we do together. Evangelists seek to minimize all that diverts attention from the focus on the crucified and risen Jesus Christ.

2. Unmediated relationships inhibit evangelical witness. When friendliness and personal connectedness become the highest value, people are forced back on themselves and drawn away from what gives life. Evangelists seek to foster relationships through Jesus Christ.

3. Primary symbols and rituals provide the means for structuring mediated relationships. Symbolic actions evoke a reality beyond the known and experienced, while presenting the ordinary stuff of life as transfigured by grace. Rituals structure what otherwise has too much power and overwhelms us. (For example: Weddings ritualize the overwhelming aspects of the marriage promise. Funerals ritualize the powerful depth of loss and grief.) Rituals also are the most effective means of unfolding communal character. The ritual life of a community shapes its practice. Evangelists carefully attend to the primary symbols and rituals of a community. But the primary symbols of the Christian community are these: the book, the water, the bread, the cup, celebrated in an inclusive and diverse community to show forth Jesus Christ.

4. The invitation to relinquish ourselves to a community is most effective when there is a common communal character. Common ritual life provides a primary way for a community of faith to unfold its character. When the "ritual of the day" or the "target-marketed" alternative worship service is designed to meet the needs of a particular group of people, the community fails to be a community. It becomes an affiliation of individuals seeking to be serviced in one way or another. A congregation with defined character both finds and expresses that character in a common ritual life. Evangelists unfold congregational character through common ritual life. But the central service, the primary ritual of the Christian community is this: we meet on Sunday, in the presence of the risen Christ, to be gathered into the life of the triune God through word and sacrament.

5. Worship continually offers the invitation to enter more deeply into Jesus Christ and the community that bears his name. Embracing the invitation

means entering a covenant. Covenants lead to transformation for both parties involved. Thus, worship itself will be continually transformed through the encounter with those who gather. Static, unchanging, and entrenched worship is not evangelical. Similarly, worship styles will vary from one context to another. While no single correct "style" of worship exists, the central shape and elements of worship cannot be viewed as one more option. Evangelists constantly listen, imagine, and risk, always with a sense of awe and respect, opening the symbolic and ritual life of the community to newness.

ABOUT THE AUTHOR

Mark A. Olson presently serves as Senior Pastor at Zion Lutheran Church, Appleton, Wisconsin. He is the founder and director of the Center for Congregational Leadership.

What is leadership in worship and evangelism?

Frank Senn

The question that serves as the title of this essay suggests two interrelated queries: What is the relationship between worship and evangelism? And what leadership is needed in worship and evangelism? As much as possible these questions will be treated together, and from the perspective of the person who should be the primary focus of the church's evangelization: the unchurched.

It is difficult for many of us, who were brought up in the church since infancy and who readily visit and expect to be welcomed as fellow believers in congregations other than our own, to put ourselves into the place of the truly unchurched person. Interviews and studies can indicate reasons why the unchurched visit churches and what they may be looking for when they do attend worship, but we cannot put ourselves into another person's stead to know with certainty what that person thought of the experience of attending worship. Nor can congregations simply replicate what other congregations have done to attract the unchurched; individual congregational dynamics, local demographics, and parish locations vary. But we do know that a congregation must be truly hospitable to strangers, that the worship service itself must be truly engaging, and that certain persons are needed who will perform specific worship ministries that promote the evangelical mission of the congregation.

Worship/music committees and evangelism

Before a worshiper ever crosses the threshold of the church building and before a liturgical minister ever enters the worship space, basic decisions must be made and planning must be done. This is usually done by committees, task forces, or planning teams. It used to be that evangelism committees and worship and music committees never interacted with one another. That is no longer possible, because people who attend a church for the first time today attend worship. Worship is the arena in which the encounter between the community of faith and the unchurched most often occurs. In this day, with a multitude of options for continuing education, recreation, support groups, and special interest groups available in our society, few unchurched people would think of coming to a church for such activities and programs unless the activity or program was simply "housed" in a church building, as many community activities and programs are. So it is worship that is most likely to attract the unchurched to "church." This fact should be welcomed as an opportunity as well as a challenge, because it means that "enquirers" or "seekers" want to experience what the church uniquely offers. Thus, the church has been given an opportunity, such as it has not had in several centuries, to proclaim and celebrate the gospel in a public way.

This situation has created an interesting new dynamic in the interaction between a congregation's evangelism and worship/music committees. The evangelism committee is likely to be concerned that public worship be dynamic, engaging, meaningful, relevant, and generally attractive to the unchurched—concerns that one hopes the worship/music committee also shares. The worship/music committee, for its part, is likely to be concerned that worship practices reflect the confessional and liturgical heritage of the community of faith—concerns that raise issues of authentic gospel proclamation and theological integrity that one hopes the evangelism committee also embraces. Nonetheless, some tension is likely between the concerns of these committees. Nothing is wrong with healthy tension in discussions about the mission of the church. Tensions here can be a way of steering a course between two common corruptions of worship: worship that is used as a tool to accomplish human ends (utilitarianism) and worship that is done only for its own sake, "for the glory of God alone," as is often claimed (aestheticism). We understand the liturgy or "public work of the people" to be both the congregation's worship of God alone and the arena in which God comes to his people through word and sacrament, and thus simultaneously God-directed and people-oriented.

Matters that will concern *both the evangelism and the worship/music committees* might include establishing worship schedules and recruiting ministers of hospitality. Matters that concern the *evangelism committee* in terms of public worship include advertising, the accessibility of the building and worship space, and follow-up with visitors. Matters that will concern the *worship/music committee* in terms of the impact of worship on visitors include the provision of capable liturgical leadership, the quality of the music, the flow of the liturgy, the adequacy of the space to facilitate the performance of the liturgy, and the provision of liturgical art that both focuses devotion and evokes response.

Attending to the particular content of individual liturgies is not something that the worship/music committee as a whole can do. But many parishes have instituted worship planning teams that normally include the pastor, the staff musicians, and assisting ministers, with opportunity for input and feedback from the worship and music committee. Items that concern the planning team include: the selection of liturgical options (e.g., canticles, hymns, prayer texts), the selection and placement of choir and instrumental music, devising a way of including the people's concerns in intercessory prayer, the content and thrust of preaching (e.g., sermons based on the lectionary readings and related to the whole liturgical celebration for the day), and the provision of a worship folder that provides information that visitors need about the congregation and the order of worship.

Ministers of hospitality

First impressions are often lasting. Therefore the first encounter with the worshiping community needs to be one of warmth and openness to strangers. The unchurched person will come to a building in which public worship is being offered, but signage will indicate that the building belongs to a private institution and the worship will be conducted according to the congregation's traditions. So both the building and the worship will be perceived ambiguously as both private and public. The unchurched person will feel this ambiguity upon arrival. It becomes especially important to put this person at ease by projecting friendliness yet avoiding unwanted intimacy, by providing interaction but preserving personal space for exploration.

The members of the congregation who extend hospitality to visitors are the first persons the visitor encounters who have a role in evangelism and worship. Many congregations now have three types of hospitality ministers: *greeters*, *ushers*, and *guides*.

Greeters should be placed at the major entrances into the building (which, in this day of parking lots, may not be the doors facing the street). These persons should be chosen for this ministry because they know the "regulars" and may look out after the needs of those who are unfamiliar with the facility. They may need to indicate how one finds the worship space, the nursery, wash rooms, Sunday school rooms, and so forth. A map of the facilities and a simple brochure listing basic information about the congregation can be given to "strangers" (including those who are "members," but attend only occasionally—after all, changes occur from one year to the next). Visitors should be asked to sign a guest book and be invited to social hours before or after the service.

Ushers usually provide worshipers with materials needed to participate in the liturgy and seat people when finding a seat becomes problematic. The term "usher," however, might be dropped in favor of "host." Such a name will convey to those who perform this ministry that hospitality rather than management of material and space is their primary task. I would further suggest that hosts be stationed where worshipers come into the narthex or vestibule, if that is possible, rather than where people enter the nave or worship space. This not only avoids congestion at the entryway into the worship space, but makes possible another task: helping people to participate more knowledgeably in the liturgy.

If the usher suspects that a visitor is unfamiliar with the worship practices of the congregation, a guide is summoned, and the next ministry of hospitality begins. The *guide* provides instruction in the use of the book. This is no time for a mini-course in liturgy. It is sufficient to indicate where the order of service begins and how hymn numbers are different from page numbers. It may be appropriate to indicate what the congregation's communion practice is. This means that those trained for this ministry must know the congregation's worship resources and sacramental practices. The guide then seats the visitors next to regular worshipers who can provide some help at various points in the liturgy and extend a further word of welcome after the service.

There is a risk that all this attention to the visitor—being greeted at the door, being equipped in the vestibule, being instructed in the nave—might be more of an intrusion than is desired by the guest. But the risk is more than outweighed by the possibility that some stranger's worship experience will be enhanced by the friendly assistance provided. More than that, the experiences of warmth at the door, of courtesy shown in the narthex, of respectful help given at the entryway and in the pew indicate a communal undertaking and create anticipation that something momentous is about to begin.

The liturgical ministers in public view

An atmosphere of hospitality, but also of anticipation, has been created. The event that takes place must exhibit an inviting quality but also a sense that something different is taking place: as an assembly, the worshipers are in the presence of God.

The liturgical ministers who may first come into public view are the *acolytes* entering the worship space and preparing for the liturgy: placing books, lighting candles, fetching processional items, and going to the place where the entrance will be formed. Acolytes are usually vested in albs, indicating their role as liturgical ministers. Acolytes need to go about their preparatory tasks with a naturalness that comes from knowing what they are doing, yet with a sense of reverence that demonstrates that something momentous is about to take place.

While the acolytes are engaged in last-minute preparations for the liturgy, *musicians* are helping to prepare people for worship. In many places, an organist is playing, but there may be other music provided by other instrumentalists or singers. Performing pre-service music must be the most difficult task for church musicians. The best of them know that they are not performing music to entertain the gathering congregation; they are doing something to help worshipers prepare for the act of worship. In the classical Lutheran tradition, the organist has usually played "preludes" on the hymns to be sung in the service. On great festivals, instrumental groups or singers might perform a pre-service selection of hymns, songs, or carols appropriate to the celebration. The gathering congregation can also be included in some of the pre-service music.

At the moment when the service begins, the *presiding minister* stands before the assembly, often to lead the Brief Order for Confession and Forgiveness as one final preparation for worship. The solemnity of this act of confession and forgiveness eschews any casualness. The presiding minister is present to lead the assembly in worship, and this should be his or her focus. The visitor will probably be more impressed by the presider who concentrates on the reason for the gathering, rather than confusing the purpose of the assembly by exuding a phony warmth toward the worshipers (and often making his or her own personality the focus of attention in the process) or making many announcements that have nothing to do with the liturgy that is about to be done (and making the congregation seem like a captive audience for commercials sponsored by parish organizations). Indeed, the presider's role in the entrance rite or introductory portion of the service is a limited one. She or he extends the apostolic greeting to the congregation, models attentiveness to prayer and joy in praise during the Kyrie and Canticle of Praise (the petitions and opening words of which are sung by an assisting minister or choir), and offers the strong, brief words of the Prayer of the Day. Then the presider steps aside for the reader or assisting minister who reads the biblical readings. Even the sermon is not so much a personal contribution to the liturgy as the public proclamation of the gospel (the *evangelion*) by the "public ministry" of the faith community. There, too, the presiding minister does not impose himself or herself on the congregation as though they were a captive audience for whom he or she is performing, and whose plaudits the minister seeks.

The role of the *assisting minister* also requires attention. The assisting minister or ministers will sing the petitions of the Kyrie (or another litany), sometimes the opening line of the Canticle of Praise, read the biblical readings, lead the intercessory prayers, and assist with the communion of the people. The assisting minister is communicating words and signs of life, and should convey both familiarity with these expressions at the heart of the community's life and a simple, unaffected reverence that comes from being close to holy things.

The liturgy and the congregation as witnesses to the gospel

At this point we must step away from the roles of the ministers to consider what is communicated by the liturgy itself. The church is called to participate in God's mission by proclaiming what God has done in Christ and enacting this in its own life. The church's liturgy, or "public work" (*leitourgia*), is actually its best witness to the gospel. This gospel is present in the words of forgiveness, the songs of praise, the prayers, the scripture readings, the sermon, the creed, the greeting of peace, the great thanksgiving, and the eucharistic meal itself.

The worshiping congregation or liturgical assembly witnesses to the gospel just by doing its liturgy: by singing its songs, offering its prayers, listening to the readings and sermon, exchanging the greeting of peace, and receiving the eucharistic bread and cup. Martin Luther recommended, in the statement on communion practices appended to his *Form of the Mass* (1523), that the communicants group themselves in the chancel so that they could be seen by the non-communicants. By their participation in the sacrament they were making a witness to how Christ's glorious testament met their personal needs and also strengthened the church in mission. The devotion of the people in joining in the songs and prayers and ritual acts will surely make a profound impression on unchurched visitors. St. Augustine testifies in his *Confessions* how important a factor in his own conversion was the sight of the people at worship. Even the song of a child influenced his movement toward baptism.

This dual witness of the liturgy and the congregation may lead the unchurched to make inquiry about the faith and the faith community. Such inquiry may consist of informal discussions with a pastor or lay leader or participation in an inquirers' class or group. At a point at which the unchurched person is ready to make a more serious commitment to the faith and the faith community, a process needs to be in place to lead the convert to full incorporation into the congregation. Rites of incorporation may include (1) reception into membership by letter of transfer from another congregation, (2) affirmation of baptism for those coming from another church body or who have been away from the life of the church for a long time, or (3) baptism. The baptism of adults will entail a catechumenal process. The development of a real catechumenal process makes such demands on the time and energy of the local church that it needs its own organization and ministers.

The catechumenate and its ministers

The real purpose of the catechumenal process is conversion—through God's grace, toward a life of faith, with the community of believers, in service to those in need. The word *catechumen* comes from a Greek word meaning "to sound in the ear." The content of the catechumenate—what "sounds in the ear" of one coming to baptism—has been the catechism, a handbook of basic Christianity. But since the purpose of the catechumenate is to nurture conversion, rote memorization of a catechism is not sufficient. *The catechumen is invited to hear the word of God and do it.* For this reason this process cannot be just another Christian education program. It seeks to inculcate the values of the reign of God, which may be in conflict with the values of one's society. This process of teaching-leading to baptism invites the seeker to recognize the mystery of God in human life and to turn towards the holy as that is known to us in Jesus Christ. It seeks to initiate the catechumen by stages into the community of faith in Jesus Christ crucified and risen again. A special catechetical team should be established to guide the catechumenal process: public enrollment of candidates for baptism; preparation through study, worship, and service; immediate preparation during Lent; the celebration of the sacraments of initiation at the Easter Vigil (baptism and first communion); the period of instruction in the sacraments during the Fifty Days of Easter; and the celebration of Christian vocation in the world on the Day of Pentecost.

In the Roman Catholic Rite of Christian Initiation of Adults and in the Catechumenal Process of the Episcopal Church, the bishop is the chief minister of Christian initiation and the diocese is involved. Therefore, there are liaison persons between the parish teams and the dioceses in these churches. Whether in Lutheran practice the bishop and the synod would play a role in the catechumenate remains to be determined, although the reasons for having episcopal and synodical participation are both practical and ecclesiological: most of the congregations are not up to the challenges of the catechumenate on their own and the bishop in his person establishes the unity in mission of the congregation and the whole local church. A person being initiated into the church must know in a concrete way that the body of Christ is more than the local congregation.

In any event, a *convener of the catechumenal team* is needed who will serve as a coordinator of volunteers, a supervisor of training, a liaison with the pastor and/or the bishop's office, and a communicator with the congregation. Such a person, who is likely to be a lay leader, should also receive sufficient training—probably by a diocesan or synodical committee on the catechumenate.

An *evangelist* is needed who will gather seekers into inquiry groups or classes and coordinate the presentations given by the pastor and lay teachers who participate in the groups. The pastor will answer questions about the faith and church practices and the lay persons will testify to their own faith and practice. The purpose of the inquiry sessions is simply inquiry. When someone is moved to seek baptism, enrollment in the catechumenal process then takes place.

A *catechist* (or several in a large congregation with many catechumens) is needed to lead sessions with the catechumens, those preparing for baptism. Typically, the catechumens will be dismissed from the assembly after the liturgy of the word with prayer and a blessing and will gather in their own group sessions. The catechist will lead Bible studies and story-sharing in the catechumenal group and supervise the participation of the catechumens in the social ministries of the congregation (e.g., soup kitchens, shelters, counseling centers, and so forth) or as volunteers in the social service agencies of the diocese or synod.

A *coordinator of sponsors* is needed who will recruit members of the congregation to serve as *sponsors* of the catechumens through the whole process from enrollment through initiation. The sponsors ideally will attend catechumenal sessions with their candidates and present them to the congregation at worship. Sponsors will also meet with the candidates from time to time to reflect on the experiences of the catechumenate. Sponsors are, in fact, "godparents" to the candidates for baptism, and should take this role seriously.

Members of the congregation might also be invited to provide *hospitality* at inquiry and catechumenal sessions: to welcome participants, supply refreshments, and plan receptions after the enrollment of candidates and the celebration of baptism.

A person who serves as a *liturgy coordinator* might be included on the catechumenal team who works with the pastor or bishop in planning the rituals of the catechumenate, and with assisting ministers, readers, acolytes, and altar guild members in implementing these services.

The *pastor* will serve as the spiritual director for the catechumens. Together with assisting ministers or deacons, the pastor or bishop will lead the ritual acts of enrollment, election, enlightenment (the public handing over of the Gospels, the Creed, and the Lord's Prayer), baptism, and first communion. The pastor or bishop will also deliver the homilies on the sacraments during the Easter season.

The Christian initiation of children

Much of the foregoing has concerned adults. Yet it is obvious that children are also brought into membership in the congregation through baptism, and need evangelization and faith formation just as adults do. This has traditionally been accomplished by Sunday school classes, first communion preparation, and confirmation ministries. All too often, however, a holistic approach to the Christian initiation of children does not take place. Children are not included in the whole life and mission of the church. They are sometimes not even included in public worship, but are siphoned off into a nursery or Sunday school. Most seriously, there is an assumption that children will simply "grow" into the faith and do not need "conversion," a "turning" from the world and its values to the values of the kingdom of God. What adults need, children need. And how children learn—by experience and interaction—is also a model that can be applied to adults.

As a congregation seeks to include children in its worship and life, it needs to ask itself whether it embraces children as children, and not just as little adults; whether the congregation's liturgy immerses children in the symbols and stories of the faith community, or just "preaches" to them; whether adults model for children daily participation in the mystery and work of Christ. Specifically with regard to worship, the congregation needs to ask whether its liturgy is done well enough that it teaches itself; whether the story of salvation told and celebrated in word and sacrament encourages children to identify with it and know that they are included in God's involvement with his people; whether there is liturgical art in the worship space that evokes religious imagination. What serves to engage the imagination and response of children will engage the imagination and response of adults. The Christian initiation of children is not an afterthought but the paradigm of the process. Jesus himself put a child in the midst of his disciples as a model of how the kingdom of God should be received.

If the model of Christian initiation of both children and adults is taken seriously, it will alter perceptions of what church and worship are about. The church will be regarded as a community in mission, and leadership in worship will be leadership in and for that mission.

ABOUT THE AUTHOR

The Rev. Frank Senn is pastor of Immanuel Lutheran Church of Evanston, Illinois. He is the president of The Liturgical Conference.

How does the liturgy inclusively share the Christian faith?

Jann Fullenwieder

Our question, of course, is the wrong question. The primary matter is not, in fact, how the liturgy is inclusive. The primary matter is always how the liturgy speaks Jesus Christ. For when the church speaks Jesus Christ in the liturgy, the liturgy speaks the inclusive word for any time or any place, for any world yet to come. This insight is not mere cleverness designed to grant Christians a reprieve from thinking through the questions of what we are about in corporate worship. The insight begs for quite the opposite: a renewal of critical commitment. The point is to focus the church so sharply on the primacy of Jesus Christ as the Word for all creation and for us that all we say, think, or do becomes a rhyme or echo of that speech and just so, is truly inclusive.

Who speaks to whom

The church at worship would hear Jesus. Any other goal is subsidiary at best, hopelessly timebound in the least, and perhaps, most urgently, contributes to a famine of the Word. So the church must be cautious about the question of liturgical inclusivity. Letting ourselves be preoccupied only with the inclusivity of the liturgy will fail to secure us in the mind of Christ Jesus and thus will limit us to the context of our own imaginations. Yet the crucified and risen Lord is for us the inclusivity of God. When we fasten our hearts in the one whom the liturgy speaks, namely Christ, we may have hope that our imaginations will be fixed in him and opened up by the character of God's own catholicity.

Liturgy is that event wherein we are gathered into Christ Jesus who speaks and is spoken. Our understanding of God's address to us is shaped by the account of Pentecost (Acts 2:1-42). God not only speaks to Jesus' followers but through them speaks Jesus for the life of the world. Pentecost reveals the Holy Spirit's vivid transfiguration of Jesus' ordinary followers into public witnesses. Moreover, the Pentecost story shows us the will of the Holy Spirit to be speaking Christ in diverse languages for all the nations of the earth. The event of Pentecost gives us the Pentecost principle: inspired believers are freed for speaking the gospel that translates into every tongue of every nation under heaven. God speaks Christ to believers, for believers, and through believers for for all the world to hear.

In earlier centuries the Pentecost principle was expressed by saying that the church—the baptized, worshiping assembly—is one, holy, apostolic, and catholic. Those who handed on the creeds to us used "catholic" to mean that Jesus is the Word given to the entire world, the Word given for the whole beloved diverse creation, for every time and every place. As humanity grows in understanding the world (using the natural, social, and historical sciences and the myriad ways of thinking that they reveal), so also will the church's ability to speak Christ Jesus in new ways expand. Spoken language, written language, body language, and visual language that constitute Christian liturgy as well as the symbolic ritual language of the surrounding culture—all of these forms of *word* adhere to the church's use of what is classically called word and sacrament, or Word and visible words. The Pentecost principle commits the church to reading the culture and to translating the gospel with a critically trained ear to all these ways humankind uses words. If such a wide array of tongues seems too vast to attend to, we must look again at the catholicity of Jesus.

The catholicity of Jesus

Just as with ancient Jonah under the castor bean bush, disquieted over the salvation of Ninevah, the narratives of the Gospels consistently make clear, even among those closest to Jesus, our human tendency to abhor the shocking catholicity of God. God's logic rubs us wrong. Jesus makes the wrong choices. Jesus is always welcoming the wrong ones, making the wrong exceptions, sharing the staff of life with the wrong guests, cultivating the wrong stuff for disciples, and lavishing healing on the wrong people in the politicized crowd. Left in our hands, in the hands of those who purport to follow Jesus, even our best worship practices can withhold a genuine, open, full, that is, *catholic* welcome.

All along the route to the cross—indeed, from the cross itself—just as Jesus' disciples think they have understood who Jesus is willing to include, Jesus overturns their frames of understanding and enlarges the picture. Jesus keeps including more people: the children who are listed among household property, Simon the elitist Pharisee, dwarfed Zaccheus, the woman about to be stoned to death, all those whose fists tightened around stones against the adulterous woman even as their fingers opened to let her adulterous male partner slip away, the begging Syro-Phoenician woman, and the inquisitive Samaritan woman at the well. Jesus claims as brother and sister multitudes beyond his blood mother and brothers and sisters. Jesus crosses the line to answer lepers and dialogue with demoniacs. Jesus casts aside his ritual cleanliness to reach for the flesh of the dead and dying. Jesus answers the petition of the Roman centurion and walks the public way, which gives the hemorrhaging woman access to him. He loves the rich young man and yet tells him the truth, which will make him turn away in sorrow. "Yes," Jesus says to the dying thief who begs Jesus to steal him out of death and lead him into paradise. Jesus, this catholic Jesus, is risen, alive, and knowable in the evangelical life of the church at worship. The very catholicity of Jesus impells us to find the words, in all their various forms, that tell of Christ in our time and place.

When we hear and believe that it is this extravagant Jesus who greets us with the kiss of peace in the liturgy, we realize that the question about inclusivity is never about how to reach the "outsiders" or "the others." The question of inclusivity is rather about us and how we turn away from the world. The barriers around liturgy are built by us, formed by our fears, and reinforced by our aspirations and preconceptions; it replicates the hardness of our hearts. The dismantling of barriers in liturgy begins with noticing our pinched hearts, wrinkled noses, closed hands, and narrowed eyes.

When we come together in the name of Jesus, we are called to pay attention with the catholicity of Christ. So then, there are many questions about us. How do we train ourselves to pay attention to who else is here now where we are? How do we tune our ears to the blind Bartimaeus's cry to the passing assembly? How do we train our eyes to notice the hemorrhaging woman who is sneaking up to touch the hem of the assembly? How do we teach the assembly to sit still next to the waters of Christ and listen to the genuine questions of the Samaritan woman? How do we learn to stop and lift up the children into the lap of the assembly, lay hands on them and bless them? How do we open the eye of the assembly to love the rich young person who turns away? How do we turn the heart of the assembly toward those whom we automatically discard, disregard, fail to hear, or do not even see in our particular contexts? How do we learn to halt the assembly when the bread of life in our hands has become for us stones of judgment we would use to pelt those caught up in seemingly unholy lives? How do we learn to see that the faces and needs of others mirror to us our own need?

Things to learn

We begin to learn awe, we begin to see the inspiring catholicity of Christ, by attending to the first things first. Like those who welcomed the gospel message at Pentecost, we are turned to baptism and are invited to devote ourselves to the apostles' teaching and fellowship, to the breaking of bread and the prayers (Acts 2:41-42). At the feet of these things, like Mary of Bethany at the feet of Jesus, we learn the way that is inclusive.

The first things are baptism, the holy supper, and the apostolic teaching around these things. These are the very things Jesus gives for disciple-making, those things for which the risen Christ calls in the last verses of Matthew

(28:18-20). All of Matthew is set forth as *didache*, the teaching of the meaning of Jesus Christ. So the crowning words bristle with intention, claiming that, in Jesus, disciple-making is an overwhelming yet welcoming washing, an abudant feeding for all who are hungry and thirsty. Jesus' own pattern of disciple-making is his teaching before and after the Passion and his calling of people into the presence of Israel's God by the power of the Holy Spirit.

We learn to share Christ inclusively in our liturgy by looking at these first things first. The teaching in Matthew emerges from the experience of Christ in the liturgy; it emerges from these first things. Clearly, for apostolic believers, from whose assemblies we inherit the Gospel narratives, in worship we use these first things in an encounter with the Risen One. Worship is the realization, here and now, of the life of the world yet to come. By nature, liturgy is the place where the first things of Christ's promises live. Liturgy is the present activity of the Risen One, not an activity Christians perform for themselves for their own sake. Liturgy is God acting in and upon the church, welling up and pouring down into the present a future guaranteed by Christ. Thus, apostolic, biblical theology sprang out of the worship meeting where the first things served, where the Spirit's gifts were set forth to speak Jesus.

Old, inherited language, old cultic patterns, ancient stories of the mighty acts of God by which God is known, the prophets' words that will not be in vain, ancient gestures of faith, clusters of symbols—all these riches were heaped up, crushed down, pressed out, and cracked open to yield even more truth than they had already fed to generations in Israel. The essence of these inherited things, extracted under the pressure of the cross, became Christ's first things. The immediacy of Christ in the midst of the people is encountered in the very fire in the lamps of the assembly, the very water in the baths, the very bread and wine in their mouths, the very kiss of homecoming on their faces, the very oil crowning their heads with the jewel of the cross.

The first things of Christian liturgy are givens. They are the source and standard of Christian reflection about Christ Jesus and about whatever we do in the name of Christ. These first things are living signs that form the church's liturgy not only by promising the resurrection but also by showing forth that new reality now in Christ, in the fulfillment of the church's present function as the body of Christ.

Preoccupation with the first things as the heart of the Christian assembly made for an astonishing uniformity in the apostolic faith. That faith criss-crossed the known civilization, east and west, in less than two centuries and, in less than four centuries, flowed from the synagogues of a small Jewish sect in Palestine to the marketplaces of the cities to the households of Roman Britain and Syrian Dura-Europus and finally flooded the throneroom of the emperor himself. The startling oneness of the faith spread by the early church was born of the preoccupation with first things, the givens of worship. This focus gave rise to a prevalence of two things: a liturgical catechumenate and preaching on the sacramental celebrations of the church (i.e., "mystagogia," reflection on the sacramental "mysteries").

The whole evangelical thrust of preaching and teaching, in Jerusalem and among all the nations, was that people might be led to the bath and to the table to see Christ. The water and table set out for the life of the world and the gospel calling all to come and take were both source and calling for Christians to turn to the nations. In order to speak inclusively, our liturgies must bring us into these primary things together.

First things center and reform liturgy

Christ's first things are how God chooses to include the world: through God's lavish Word, Christ, in the broken bread; through the cleansing flood; and by all these things spoken in every tongue of every nation under heaven. Sharing the simple gifts of story and promise, bread and wine, water and teaching, according to the practice of Jesus—that is how we share the faith inclusively. These first things, and our taking them up in thanksgiving, are Jesus' promised self-giving.

Because we are given this way into Christ who is all in all, it behooves the church to share the faith inclusively by lifting up steadfastly these given sources of the faith. Our considered use of the first things holds the assembly open to the world and commits us to paying attention to the world. These first things, used in the Spirit and informed by the Pentecost principle, bring us face-to-face with the blind Bartimaeus in our path and skin-to-skin with the leper of our day. Christ's first things act as the reforming heart of the body of Christ. Because these things together speak Christ, because they mutually interpret and echo one another, they model for us God's inclusive vision. There is no other place to look for a way to understand God's surprising catholicity.

Guests are not hosts

"The grace of our Lord Jesus Christ, the love of God, and the communion of the Holy Spirit be with you all," says the presider. "And also with you," responds the assembly. In these or similar words, we are called into the liturgy. Even as this exchanged greeting announces the meaning of the event, it also names the one into whom we are gathered. We are gathered face-to-face into the hospitable Trinity, according to the love of God, by the grace of Jesus, in the unity of the Spirit of God.

Perhaps if we see the gracious Christ as the host of the liturgy, it will be clear to us that we are among those who are gathered in from the wayside and the highways and the bushes and the back alleys. At Christ's feast, at any Christian service of worship, the event is not our occasion. It is not our freedom to choose the guests nor to determine who is to be included. Our freedom for hospitality in liturgy is never the sovereign freedom of the host. Our freedom for one another, our courtesy, is derivative from our being hospitably gathered. Ours is the kind charity, the benevolent favor, the considerate compassion of a guest among a company of guests. Even if we could say somehow that we were first, we still number among all those before whom the gates of heaven are thrown eternally wide, that we might enter together into the presence of God.

We are guests. Moreover, despite all appearances, despite all the powerfully positive thinking we visit upon ourselves, we are, so to speak, the guests who invariably show up late, who have dirt under our nails, who speak in accents of the wrong region, who have the manners of the ill-bred, who wear the wrong tie, who sport a dress infinitely too casual for the occasion, who exhale a fetid breath, and who laugh too loud. Most often, we are the elder son, the one who was here first and who has stayed around longest. We think we understand who we are and who the others are in relationship to God. We are just as confused as our younger brother, the prodigal son who believes that all that is left to hope for is some shred of subsistence. We are together the guests who confuse the father's welcome. *The father's welcome*, the humble, unhesitating, joyous running of the ancient head to gather in and embrace the beloved, broken, and unwashed, is what is at stake in our liturgies.

So the seventeenth-century English poet George Herbert wrote:

> Love bade me welcome yet my soul drew back,
>   Guilty of dust and sin.
> But quick-eyed Love, observing me grow slack
>   From my first entrance in,
> Drew nearer to me, sweetly questioning,
>   If I lacked anything.
> A guest, I answered, worthy to be here:
>   Love said, You shall be he.

We are guests. We are among those whom quick-eyed Love chooses to welcome. Ours is to sit and eat and open our eyes to how long and how wide and how laden the table is, stretching from before the world began, twisting through all tribes and peoples, and reaching out over the river at the end of time.

For us gathered at this table the matter becomes that of passing on the food. Or, in liturgy our concern will be helping our neighbor understand what the food is, and making sure that when the water comes we fill the cups of those who are thirsty and wash the feet of those who need to be cleansed and refreshed. They will be drawn in by the great swell of song rising from the guests. For us to be guests is to learn to gaze upon all who surround us and to behold them as beloved, as welcomed as we are, our astonished selves.

Who is not heard

Worship centers us deeply in the astonishing, catholic hospitality of God, welcomes us into Christ's first things, and impels us in this very Spirit to heed the world's voices. Yet this inclusive event occurs in the limited languages of human gesture and discourse. So we immediately ask of our common praise and prayer, "Who is not heard in this liturgy?" The silenced voices expose ways our actions and words gag, distort, and garble the speaking of God's first things. Silenced voices herald guests we prefer to ignore. Mute voices articulate the current oddness of God's hospitality. Here, then, is an initial list for training our attention to voices unheard:

Is Jesus heard? That is, do we honor as primary Christ's first things? Are our liturgies formed from the opening of biblical narratives, the lifting of the world before God, the washing into Christ, and the eating and drinking of Christ's mercy? Does the preacher speak for us this day the Christ of these things?

Are the witnesses who have gone before us heard? That is, do we acknowledge that we worship with and hand on what was first given to us? Is our practice enlivened and corrected by a historical awareness and a sense that our faith is communal by nature, not an invention for ourselves?

Are the baptized heard? That is, do the practices, language, and uses in our worship honor the baptismal worth of all the people, whatever their age, condition, or class? Are differing gifts and ministries recognized in a shared leadership of worship that recognizes Christ's authority granted within the body, not simply deposited in a single office? Are children welcome here and are their gifts welcome among the liturgical ministers? Are older adults similarly welcome? Women and men? Gay and lesbian and straight? Black and white? Do our spaces, our music, our art, and our vestments serve to collect a gathering of both unacquainted and familiar people into Christ and bring them into the first things? Or do these secondary things mark a hierarchy of "holiness" or national pride or divisions of race and class?

Are the inquirers heard? That is, does our liturgy stand at the heart of a teaching practice that takes seriously the questions of the inquirer, the struggles of the faithful to translate Christ in their lives, and the daily return to the first things? Does the preacher unfold the mysteries to relate them to actual hearers' questions? Does a liturgical catechumenate surround baptism and ground parish life and mission?

Are those to whom Jesus listens heard? That is, does our liturgy acknowledge and speak to the stranger, the unemployed, the despairing, the poor, the "bum," the enemy officer, those with aching hearts? Do our homilies, prayers, and patterns of welcome only acknowledge what is acceptable in our sight? Does our language conjure up private, interior worlds or address the whole, public world, the great context of living? Are the first things set out with such largeness that they are intriguing to everyone?

Are strangers heard? That is, do planners intentionally invite strangers to offer critical reflections on the action and event of the local liturgy? Do we regularly question our hearers whether what is spoken is heard, if what is enacted is seen? Do we inquire about what distorts the intended message? Do we attend, in this regard, to the language of space, gesture, ritual, music, and sign?

Is the situation heard? That is, does denominational and local liturgical practice recognize the moment, the place, and the particular people engaged in worship? Do planners search for the best contemporary liturgical language to speak Christ and his first things? Do we press into service significant local commemorations, traditions, metaphors, and idioms to speak Christ?

Is the whole world heard? That is, does our liturgy acknowledge that the creation is made new in the rising of Christ? Does the liturgy speak a love for the whole creation? Does our inclusivity apply solely to humans, leaving the richness of God's creatures, moons, and wild gardens under the oppressive whim of voracious human appetites?

Is the silence heard? That is, are there sufficient spaces to evoke what does not come to expression, to welcome mystery?

"I am with you always," the risen Lord says. Paraphrasing Matthew 28, we may hear him saying, "I am with you always in your attempt to teach, wash, and welcome into my first things." Yet without one thing, these first things given to the church to speak Christ will be distorted. For the cross breaks open all these things as God's mercy poured out to all people in so many different situations, to people and circumstances we cannot even imagine. Set next to the cross, the great I AM gives us the first things to speak Christ for the life of the world. Taking up these awesome gifts, the church beseeches, "O God, make us set them forth in the light of the cross, in the pattern of the identity of Jesus." Only then will we share the truly stunning, catholic, faithful God.

ABOUT THE AUTHOR

The Rev. Jann Fullenwieder teaches worship at Lutheran Theological Seminary in Saskatoon, Saskatchewan.

AFTERWORD

Some contemporary proposals for evangelism have invited the local church to pour its efforts into attention to the needs of "outsiders." Many of these proposals have then made a great distinction between "seekers" and "believers," generally counseling that Sunday worship should be seeker-oriented and that the needs of believers should be satisfied at another time.

In the face of such proposals, we have read Senn, Olson, and Fullenwieder. Senn reminds us that our own children, participants already in many facets of the life of the church, are in need of evangelization. Olson proposes that evangelical activity is appropriately addressed to everyone, inside and outside the congregation. In this need, there is no "us" and "them." And Fullenwieder makes clear that all of us are guests, radically in need of the great mercy of the "host" who is God.

These are wise words. From the perspective of the deepest Reformation theology, every Christian is always being called, again and again, to faith. Faith is never something I have forever. I always need the word coming from outside of me, mediated in the word of my sister and brother, alive in the community, given to me to eat and drink in the supper, washed over me in the remembrance of my baptism in order to believe. I am not, forever, a "believer." I am a seeker with all seekers, an outsider with all outsiders, a beggar with all beggars. In fact, when we tell the truth about our need of God and about God's astonishing mercy to us in the crucified and risen Christ, we are the more free to identify with outsiders rather than distinguish ourselves from them. We need to ask Jann Fullenwieder's hard questions about whether our congregation is actually doing that, but it will be the wrong answer to propose that we insiders can be fed at another time.

For we have only the central means of the grace of God to speak that truth about God's mercy. We have only the word and the sacraments with which to do evangelism. They are our only means to tell the truth about God, and, so, the truth about ourselves. If we center some service of worship intended for outsiders on anything else—on our own ideas of moral uplift, practical help, or spiritual entertainment, for example—we will not be telling the truth. We will not be setting out the very means that God gives us to enable faith. *Our confessional commitment to word and sacraments must actually show in our communal life.* For we have nothing else—nothing that is really bread instead of a stone—to give, both to our utter need and to the utter need of our neighbor, the newcomer.

The community of Christians is *baptized*. But all of us come again and again, throughout our life, at every baptism of a new Christian, at every baptismally-based word of absolution, at every preaching of Christ, at every teaching of grace, at every encounter with the holy supper, back to our own baptism. We are made alive again, together with Christ. We are formed anew into his one body. *This baptism*—and the word that accompanies it and the supper to which it leads—*is what we have to give to any seeker*. Then we must not hide it. It must be at the center of what we do. Our evangelism, if it is to tell the truth about Christ and not just be a program for "our" new members, must be entirely baptismal.

Then it is no wonder that these writers have given us a sacramental, liturgical evangelism.

And it is no wonder that the next book in this series will be about baptism. Join us in that next discussion of the open questions.

Gordon Lathrop

FOR FURTHER READING

Brueggemann, Walter. *Biblical Perspectives on Evangelism: Living in a Three-Storied Universe.* Nashville: Abingdon, 1993.

Hanson, Paul D. *The People Called: The Growth of Community in the Bible.* San Francisco: Harper and Row, 1986.

Kiefert, Patrick R. *Welcoming the Stranger: A Public Theology of Worship and Evangelism.* Minneapolis: Fortress, 1992.

Ludolph, Frederick P. *Living Witnesses: The Adult Catechumenate: Preparing Adults for Baptism and Ministry in the Church.* Winnipeg: Evangelical Lutheran Church in Canada, 1992.

Olson, Mark A. *The Evangelical Pastor: Pastoral Leadership for a Witnessing People.* Minneapolis: Augsburg Fortress, 1992.

Olson, Mark A., and Brian Burchfield. *An Evangelizing People: Lay Leadership for a Witnessing People.* Minneapolis: Augsburg Fortress, 1992.

Senn, Frank C. *The Witness of the Worshiping Community: Liturgy and the Practice of Evangelism.* Mahwah, N.J.: Paulist, 1993.

Webber, Robert E. *Liturgical Evangelism: Worship as Outreach and Nurture.* Harrisburg, Pa.: Morehouse, 1986.